# Thinking About Our Faith

## A Guide and Workbook for Growing and Learning

by Oral Withrow

*Second Edition*

**Study Guide for Theology for Disciples**

for Individuals · Groups · Pastors · Lay Leaders

Warner Press

Anderson, Indiana

Warner Press
Connect • Equip • Inspire

Published by Warner Press Inc.
Warner Press and the "WP" logo are trademarks of Warner Press Inc.



Warner Press Inc.
PO Box 2499
Anderson, IN 46018-2499
800-741-7721
www.warnerpress.org

ISBN-13: 978-1-59317-613-6

Printed in the United States of America.

LSI—POD

# CONTENTS

# INTRODUCTION

Dr. Gilbert Stafford has provided an excellent resource for the Church of God in his book ***Theology for Disciples.*** He helps us think about our faith in ways that strengthen our spiritual life and our commitment to Christ. A professor of theology in the Seminary of Anderson University, an experienced pastor, and for ten years, the speaker for Christians Broadcasting Hope, the radio voice of the Church of God, Dr. Stafford is uniquely qualified to lead us in our thoughts about God and his ways.

His book is a long one and many will want to read every page. Other persons will want to use the book as a **resource**; its **Contents** and **Subject Index** make it a valuable tool for quick reference. Still others, for a variety of reasons, will not choose to read the book. They do, however, want to explore their faith, often in the company of other disciples, using the insights and challenge of Dr. Stafford.

This **workbook** is prepared both for those who want to think about their faith "at a beginning level" and for those who want to pursue a more serious study of their beliefs. For each session, two sets of activities and questions are provided. **Experiments in Theology** is particularly useful with Sunday school classes and small groups. **Explorations in Theology** will provide challenge for persons called to be pastors, associate pastors, and lay leaders.

The page numbers for quotations from *Theology for Disciples* **are in parenthesis**. All page numbers refer to the second edition. No attempt is made to provide references or list resources, information which is generously provided by footnotes in *Theology for Disciples.*

Several words are in **bold print** to facilitate quick reading during discussions and provide emphasis to assist the individual learner in his or her study. Occasionally quotes are formatted for emphasis. Quotations from *Theology for Disciples* are provided on the first several pages of each study segment.

**A Leader's Guide** is provided which will assist the teacher with ideas for prompting discussion-experimenting with and exploring theology.

Teachers and group leaders, especially potential lay leaders and pastors, will benefit from a reading of *God's Redeeming Story* by Merle D. Strege and Richard L. Willowby and *God as Loving Grace* by Barry L. Callen, along with *Theology for Disciples.*

### EXPERIMENTS AND EXPLORATIONS

Two workbook sessions are provided for each subject, after two pages of selected quotes:

**(1) Experiments in Theology**—activities and questions particularly for disciples in small groups and Sunday school classes, and other growing Christians;

**(2) Explorations in Theology**—activities and questions especially for disciples called or aspiring to serve as leaders in the church, including teachers, elders, and pastors.

A group leader or a person studying alone may choose, of course, to select activities and questions from both pages. Questions do not necessarily have a "right" answer; the activities and questions encourage a process of thinking about our faith.

Persons preparing for a vocational ministry, for instance to be a pastor, are encouraged to do both the Experiments in Theology and Explorations in Theology.

CHAPTER 1

# DISCIPLES: THINKING ABOUT OUR FAITH

## Disciples

The essence of church life is discipleship. Disciples are learners. The church is a community of learners at the feet of Christ Jesus. Regardless of how long we have been in the church and regardless of what office we may hold, we should continue thinking of ourselves as learners (xix).

## Crucial Issue: Church as Circle of Disciples

The crucial issue is whether a church actually functions first and foremost as a circle of the Lord's disciples (regardless of its traditional identification), or, first and foremost as a bureaucracy or as an arena of emotionalism (12).

## Theology for Participation in the Whole Church

The day for narrowly conceived, denominationally oriented theologies is over. While my roots are deep in the Church of God (Anderson), they are not therein root bound; they extend into the rich heritage of the whole church. It used to be that when I appreciated something about another tradition of the Christian faith, I wished it were mine as well. No longer is that the case. I now embrace it as mine (xxi).

## Systematic Theology

Many church members relate to the Christian faith as though it were a jigsaw puzzle never put together. They have a piece called the Spirit, another called the return of the Lord, another called creation, and other pieces called the virgin birth, baptism, Jesus Christ, prophecy, healing, the Lord's supper, redemption, worship, resurrection, sanctification, as well as many others (21).

**Systematic theology** is an attempt to put the pieces together so that people can see the faith more as a whole and discover new dimensions of meaning in it (21).

Why, then, the discipline of systematic theology? It is so that preachers, teachers, and other officers and leaders in the life of the church may both reflect analytically on the content of what they preach, teach, and do, and develop in themselves and others a deeper appreciation for that content as a whole (20).

The word *theology* comes from two Greek words, *theos,* God, and *logos,* word or reason. The Latin form of this combination is *theologia,* discourse about God (18).

First, theology refers to a particular thinker's formalized position regarding matters of faith. Usually this normalization takes place through the writing of books.... (18).

Second, theology refers to a school of thought within the church's intellectual history. [For instance: Lutheran, Reformed, Wesleyan theologies; or liberal, conservative, neo-orthodox, process, or narrative theologies; also feminist, liberation, and black theologies] (18).

Third, theology refers to a discipline of critical analysis [examples are biblical theology, natural or philosophical theology, historical, dogmatic, spiritual, practical or applied or pastoral] (19).

### Truth, Creeds, Confessions, Doctrines, Dogmas, Catachesis

**Truth** is what we believe to be the case for all regardless of the perceptions others may have. To illustrate this with a nonreligious example, let us consider one who thinks that she can fly from one skyscraper to another a block away unaided by any mechanical devices. If a beloved relative were to attempt that, it is doubtful that one would say, "What is true for me may not be true for you." It is more likely that one would plead with the loved one not to pursue what would be viewed as a misconception (196).

**Creeds** are concise statements of Christian belief used primarily in worship to give witness to the historical faith as over against some heresy. The word comes from the Latin *credo* meaning "I believe"... (17).

**Confessions** are formal statements of the beliefs held by a particular group of Christians (17).

**Doctrines** are extensively argued positions widely held by the church (e.g., the doctrine of the virgin birth) or by a particular segment of the church (e.g., the doctrine of entire sanctification subsequent to justification and prior to glorification) (18).

**Dogmas** are truth declarations promulgated by an ecclesiastical body about the way things really are. Such truth, therefore, is understood to have universal applicability regardless of whether all agree with it (18).

**Catechesis** is a form of instruction that uses the method of questions and answers both of which are determined by the instructor (22).

## SCRIPTURES

**Disciples:**

Matthew 5:1-11
Matthew 28:16-20
Mark 1:16-20; 2:13-14

**Theology:**

Luke 24:13-32
John 14:1-7
2 Timothy 2:15; 3:14-17
1 Peter 3:15
Revelation 1:9-11

## NOTES

## EXPERIMENTS IN THEOLOGY

*Activities and questions particularly for disciples in small groups and Sunday school classes, and other growing Christians. Use additional pages if needed.*

Three-year-old Brady asked his mother to close the blinds when he was put to bed one night explaining, "I don't want Jesus watching me while I sleep." The previous day Brady's Sunday school teacher had talked to him and others about God's care for us.

What are some of the earliest ideas about God, Jesus, and the Holy Spirit that you remember from your childhood?

______________________________

______________________________

______________________________

______________________________

______________________________

______________________________

Ask two or three others to recall their first concepts of God with you.

Write what you believe to be the three principle characteristics of a disciple of Jesus Christ. (Or, you may discuss with another.) It may be difficult to limit your list to just three characteristics.

1. ______________________________
2. ______________________________
3. ______________________________

Systematic theology is an attempt to take all the various things we believe and "put the pieces together so that people can see faith more as a whole."

State four or five things which you believe. What things do you believe which do not seem to fit in neatly with your other beliefs?

______________________________

______________________________

______________________________

## EXPLORATIONS IN THEOLOGY

*Activities and questions especially for disciples called or aspiring to serve as leaders in the church, including teachers, elders, pastors. Use additional pages if needed.*

Read Chapter 1, "Disciples Making Disciples," and Chapter 2, "Disciples Thinking about Their Faith," in *Theology for Disciples.*

Ask three Christian leaders, at least one of them a pastor, to briefly summarize his or her beliefs about God, life, and eternity. Write below your understanding of their answers:

1. ______________________________
2. ______________________________
3. ______________________________

What Christian disciplines have been the easiest for you to learn and put into practice? What Christian disciplines have caused you the most difficulty (either in your thinking or putting them into practice)?

Easiest ______________________________

______________________________

Most difficult ______________________________

______________________________

In three sentences or less, explain, in a way and with words a new Christian will understand, what it means to be a disciple of Jesus Christ.

______________________________

______________________________

______________________________

Write below one sentence with which you would (presently) begin your own statement of a systematic theology.

______________________________

______________________________

______________________________

______________________________

CHAPTER 2

# The Book

## The Bible, A Book of Faith

The **Bible** provides the autobiography of the pioneer people of God in their pilgrimage of faith (29).

What makes the Bible different is that it conveys God's **faith-inducing revelation** generation after generation. As such, it is not only the book of God's people but the Holy Spirit's book (31).

In Scripture we have the **eternal word** in the **literary word** so that we can experience the **transforming word** leading to newness of life (40).

## Hebrew and Christian Scriptures

The Hebrew scriptures were seen by the Christian community not as crusty literary antiques from the religious past, but as lively, vibrant literary instruments of the contemporary gospel. In fact, it was to these very scriptures that 2 Timothy 3:15 refers as being "able to instruct you for salvation through faith in Christ Jesus" (30).

Over the course of some three centuries, the church's foundational body of literary works—which we know as the **New Testament**—came into existence as an extension of the Hebrew scriptures. The Christian scriptures, including the Old and New Testaments, are the only authoritative record we have of the faith of God's people from the beginning of time to the fullness of time. Though written across many centuries by numerous persons, under all sorts of circumstances and for multiple purposes, the Bible emerged with a story line stretching all the way from creation to the consummation of Israel's history in Jesus Christ and pointing to the consummation of world history at the end of the age.

As the book of a particular people, it is, therefore a historical document that lends itself to historical, literary, and sociological analysis. If the church is to be faithful to itself as a people of historical process, there is no logical option other than to encourage such critical investigation (30–31).

## Theories of the Inspiration of Scripture

This gives rise to the conviction that these writings, experienced as being divinely inspired by the original hearers and readers, are experienced by us also as being divinely inspired. To say that they are divinely inspired is to say that in them and through them we hear God speaking to us in a definite way (31).

*Major View No.1.* The theory of verbal inspiration (having to do with words) holds that each word of Scripture originated with God so that all the writers as instruments of God, though using words, sentences, and concepts that were native to them, were actually giving forth the divine words of God in the original act of speaking and writing (33).

*Major View No.2.* The theory of plenary (full) inspiration holds that while the words and thought forms belong to the writers, the message itself is fully God's. The literary form which that message takes is that of the writers who were indeed sensitive to the direction of the Spirit but were nevertheless functioning as people of their own age and place as they gave expression to the divine message inspired in their hearts and minds (33).

*Major View No.3.* The Theory of dynamic inspiration (having to do with change and growth) hold that those who wrote the books of the Bible were in a lively, growing faith relationship with God and that as God worked in, through and with them, they grew in their understanding of God (34).

Verbal inspiration places the emphasis on the words of Scripture, plenary inspiration on its message, and dynamic inspiration on the faith relationship that produced it. The difference between the three has to do with whether it is the individual words and sentences that are God-breathed or the central message or the faith of the writers (34–35).

Regardless of these differing emphases, however, in all three of these views, the same conviction holds, namely, that the Bible is the literary location where God continues to speak to us for the purpose of bringing us to faith and offering us newness of life (35).

### The Christian Scripture Principle

In short, the Christian scripture principle is that those writings are scripture that are

1. experienced by the church at large as being inspired of God,
2. accepted by the church at large as being sacred writings,
3. instructive for salvation through faith in Jesus Christ, and
4. useful for the purpose of instructing, judging, aligning, and shaping the people of God so that they will come to be and do what God wants them to be and do.

The sixty-six books of the Bible are the books so accepted by the church as a whole (Catholic, Orthodox, and Protestant) as meeting all four of these criteria (37–38).

The Bible as authoritative scripture must be allowed to stand as it is, with Christ at its center integrating all the parts and shedding light on the whole. With all of its diversity, ambiguity, and textual conundrums, the Bible must be translated and transmitted in the public arena so that its multiplicity—a multiplicity which God evidently approves—is preserved for the church's edification. In fact, the unity of the church depends on its willingness to embrace the multiplicity found in Scripture and to profit from it (39).

## SCRIPTURES

2 Timothy 3:14–17
Jeremiah 1:4
Hebrews 1:1–4
Exodus 31:18
Revelation 1:9–11

**NOTES**

## EXPERIMENTS IN THEOLOGY

*Activities and questions particularly for disciples in small groups and Sunday school classes, and other growing Christians. Use additional pages if needed.*

Read the following scripture portions and then state one belief that is created or influenced by each scripture:

Genesis 22:1–14 ______________________________

Exodus 3:1–6 ______________________________

Isaiah 40:3–5 ______________________________

Mark 1:9–15 ______________________________

Romans 12:1–2 ______________________________

Revelation 2:1–7 ______________________________

Give the **popular name,** a name sometimes used in the church and in our culture, for the following scriptures:

Genesis 1:1–5 ______________________________

Psalm 23 ______________________________

Matthew 5:1–11 ______________________________

Matthew 24:36–39 ______________________________

John 3:16 ______________________________

Matthew 28:19–20 ______________________________

1 Corinthians 13 ______________________________

Hebrews 11 ______________________________

What do each of these scriptures teach us about our faith? ______________________________

______________________________

______________________________

______________________________

What are the various ways, privately or in a group, that we may read the Bible?

Of all the ways of reading the Bible, which one or two are best for you?

Do you believe the sixty-six books of the Bible are uniquely an expression of God and have meanings for our Christian faith more than any other writings? If so, why?

## EXPLORATIONS IN THEOLOGY

*Activities and questions especially for disciples called or aspiring to serve as leaders in the church, including teachers, elders, pastors. Use additional pages if needed.*

Read chapter 3, "The Church's Book of Faith," in *Theology for Disciples.*

Three **theories of inspiration** of the scriptures are identified in *Theology for Disciples.* Summarize them below and then state what you believe about the inspiration of the books of the Bible.

1. ______________________________
2. ______________________________
3. ______________________________

I believe:

______________________________

______________________________

Explain, in a way a teenage Christian will understand, what we mean when we say, "The Bible is 'The Church's Book of Faith!'"

______________________________

______________________________

State below four observations about the Bible you would make speaking to a class or preaching a sermon; assume you are encouraging an increased appreciation for the Bible and a commitment to regular reading of the scriptures.

1. ______________________________
2. ______________________________
3. ______________________________
4. ______________________________

What scriptures do you have difficulty accepting "as a word from the Lord?" What scriptures do you believe to be best for instructing and inspiring disciples?

______________________________

______________________________

CHAPTER 3

# The Biblical God

## How Do I Know There Is a God?

### *Four Classical Arguments*

1) The **ontological** argument, as set forth by Anselm of Canterbury (1033–1109), argues ... God is that beyond which nothing greater can be conceived. Since to exist is greater than nonexistence, God must exist...

2) The **cosmological** approach, an argument made by Thomas Aquinas (c. 1225–74), argues on the basis of causation. Since everything must have a sufficient cause in order to exist and since the world does not possess within itself any causation sufficient to explain the existence of the whole, there must be, then, a sufficient cause beyond the world that brought it into existence, namely God.

3) The **teleological** approach argues that nature has design and purpose, and therefore must have a designer, i.e., God [Thomas Aquinas, William Paley (1743–1805, and Peter Bertocci; the latter speaks of "purposeful interrelatedness"].

4) The moral approach, the classical proponent being Immanuel Kant (1724–1804), argues on the basis of apparent universality of a sense of obligation to others, which points to a source of ought common to all (43–44).

## The God of the Bible

The Bible begins with none of these questions [Proving the existence of God, Where is God when I need help? and What is God like?], (44).

The God of the Bible **calls us to faithful participation in the divine mission** in the world. In Scripture, this theme predominates over questions about God' existence, lamentations about God's absence, and abstract discussions about God's nature (45).

### Three Ways to Speak of the Biblical God

1. God Initiates Conversation and **Calls Us to Communion** [Gen. 1:3, 28; 2:16–20; 3:1–5].
2. God Comes to Where We Are and **Calls Us to Faith** [Gen. 12:1, 17:1–2; 22:1–13] ... People of biblical faith are those who, upon hearing the call of God, respond, like Abraham, in trust and obedience (see Rom. 4 and 9, Gal. 3, Heb. 11, and James 2).
3. God Takes Us By Surprise and **Calls Us to Mission** [Exodus 3; also Acts 1–2] (46–47).

### God the Eternal Missionary

The God of the Bible is the **eternal missionary** who comes to earth to establish the kingdom of heaven and to **incorporate us** into the missionary venture This is a radically different kind of deity than typically is found in either religious or philosophical history where the gods are thought of either as humans blown large or as stupendous mysteries disconnected from the daily circumstances of life (49).

### God and Biblical Salvation

*First,* biblical salvation is a matter of hearing the call of God and responding to it in faith (50).

*Second,* the church is called to be faithfully involved in the ongoing mission of God in Christ [Luke 24:47–48] (50).

*Third,* the biblical God is neither subject alone nor predicate alone. God is a sentence..... The subject God and the predicate of God's mission in the world are inextricably tied together in the Bible (50).

### Holy God, Holy Call, Holy Mission, Holy Newness

Ours is the holy God who issues a holy call for us to participate in a holy mission to create holy newness. We come to know God as we respond in faith to God's call, move out in God's power on God's mission and open ourselves continually to God's eternal newness. God is the dynamic one who shatters all rigidities. God is the moving one who defies all narrow, conceptual confinements. God is the living one who abandons all dead religion. God is the personal subject who supersedes all philosophical, theological, and dogmatic objectifications. In reply to all questions about God, the eternal I AM WHO I AM still bids us to tell them that I AM has sent me to you" (51).

## SCRIPTURES

Genesis 1:1
Exodus 3:1-15
John 4:21-24
Acts 17:22-31

### NOTES

## EXPERIMENTS IN THEOLOGY

*Activities and questions particularly for disciples in small groups and Sunday school classes, and other growing Christians. Use additional pages if needed.*

Several images affect our understanding of and relationship with God. A few of the images are:

| | | | |
|---|---|---|---|
| Father | Savior | Judge | Dad |
| Creator | All-knowing | Friend | Capricious |
| Spirit | Wise Old Man | George Burns | Love |
| Miracle Worker | | | |

What other images (or descriptions) come to your mind? ______________________

______________________________________________________________

Which images of God are most comfortable for you? ______________________

______________________________________________________________

Which images reflect more nearly the biblical concepts of God? ______________________

______________________________________________________________

Complete this sentence: I believe in God because...

______________________________________________________________

Ask three persons in your group, class, or family to complete the same sentence and then compare your comments.

- ______________________________________________________
- ______________________________________________________
- ______________________________________________________

Dr. Stafford says that God "Calls Us to Communion," "Calls Us to Faith," and "Calls Us to Mission." How and when have you experienced the call of God in your life?

______________________________________________________________

______________________________________________________________

## EXPLORATIONS IN THEOLOGY

*Activities and questions especially for disciples called or aspiring to serve as leaders in the church, including teachers, elders, pastors. Use additional pages if needed.*

Read chapter 4, "The Biblical God," in *Theology for Disciples.*

In a small group meeting in a home one woman said, "I don't prove God, I just believe in him." A man across the room agreed but, as he explained, "With some reservations. As far back as I can remember I have believed God exists and have found no reason to question it!"

The faith and experience of both of these persons is meaningful and there is no reason to question the validity of their faith. So, is it important for them to be able to state reasons for believing there is a God? Why?

Were you to be asked to give an argument (statement) proving the existence of God, which one of the four classical arguments would you prefer to use? Would you prefer to use another type of statement for "proving" there is a God?

Summarize either the classical argument you prefer, or, make your own statement about the existence of God.

God calls us! Dr. Stafford speaks of three ways that God calls us: to communion, to faith, and to mission.

Are these calls different and separate encounters with God or, are they all a part of each other? Do they come in any certain order? Is it possible to respond to one or two of these calls in a positive way but negatively to one of them?

God said to Moses, "I AM WHO I AM" (Exodus 3:14). What is the meaning of that scripture? Does it help you in your understanding of faith? Does the phrase make rational belief in God more difficult for you? Ask a pastor or lay leader about his or her understanding of this biblical phrase.

## CHAPTER 4

# CHRIST AND THE KINGDOM

### The Lord of *All* Creation

**Creation** is the **arena** of the Kingdom,
**history** is the **drama** of the Kingdom,
**Christ** is the **essence** of the Kingdom,
the **church** is the **community** of the Kingdom.
Individual **believers** are **agents** of the Kingdom and
the **return of Christ** will usher in the **consummation** of the Kingdom.
(54, formatted for emphasis)

The **human order** and the **rest of creation** are viewed not as two independent realms but as mutually interpenetrating ones (54).

When sinners are converted, believers are sanctified and the people of God live in the power of the Spirit, the **whole created order joins in songs of praise**. According to Revelation 4 and 5 heavenly worship includes the whole created order joining in triumphant hymns of adoration (55).

Consequently, there is **no dissonance** between what Christ does on the historical plane and what he does in relation to the whole created order. The one Lord is creator, redeemer, and sustainer both of his people and of the whole of creation. He is both particularly and uniquely present among his people and universally and pervasively present in creation. The God, then, who works among God's people, is none other than the God who is also the cohesive substructure of creation (56).

### The Kingdom and the Church: Comparisons

The church came into existence with the conviction that in Jesus of Nazareth what had been prophetically promised was now a reality. He was the perfect citizen, the promised messiah, the new environment, and the victor over all that opposes God (59).

Paul's treatment of the **new environment** is our **being in Christ.** Second Corinthians 5:17: "So if anyone is in Christ, there is a new creation: everything old has passed away; see, everything has become new!" In fact the whole Book of Ephesians is a treatise on the newness that belongs to those who are in Christ (65).

In that the **church** is the community of Jesus Christ, it is thereby the **community of the Kingdom**. Even though the church, while being the body of Christ is not Christ, likewise, though it is the community of the Kingdom it is not synonymous with the Kingdom (68).

> Kingdom comes from God (Matt. 6:10; Luke 11:2)
> Church is built by Jesus (Matt. 16:18)
> Kingdom is a qualitative reality (Rom. 14:7)
> Church is a quantitative reality (Matt. 28:19)
> Kingdom is the reign and rule of God, free of all human frailties (John 18:36)
> Church submits to the reign and rule of God but is not free of the frailties of human participation (Eph. 2:20)
> Kingdom grows by grace and not at all by human strategy (John 3:3)
> Church grows by grace and human strategy (Acts 1: 8)
> Kingdom will be consummated at the end of the age (1 Cor. 15:24)
> Church will be gathered for the consummation of the Kingdom (1 Thess. 4:1–7).
> (68–69, formatted for emphasis)

The church as the community of the Kingdom **prays** for the **coming** of the Kingdom, **grows** in the **qualities** of the Kingdom, **trusts** in the **Lord** of the Kingdom, **rejoices** in the **spread** of the Kingdom and **looks forward** to the **consummation** of the Kingdom (69).

Our conclusion is that each believer is to become in human history a personalized expression of the presence of the Kingdom (71).

### *Parousia* (Coming)

The consummation of this world order at the time of the *parousia* [coming of the Lord] will manifest to the whole world not only the **lordship of Jesus Christ** but also the fact that **Satan** is a **defeated** foe. This is the theme of the Book of Revelation (73).

Jesus, as the Lord of the consummation of this world order makes cosmic display of the kingdom of God, which is grandly described in Revelation 21–22:7 as

- "a new heaven and a new earth"
- "the holy city, the new Jerusalem, coming down to of heaven from God, prepared as a bride adorned for her husband" ... (75).

The Kingdom in consummation will be an eternal sanctuary where the people of the lamb will worship their Lord face to face and reign with him forever and ever [Rev. 22:3–5] (75).

## SCRIPTURES

Colossians 1:15–17
Hebrews 9:11–12; 12:22–24
Revelation 1:7
Romans 8:19–22
Matthew 24:27–31
1 Corinthians 15:52
1 Thessalonians 4:16

**NOTES**

## EXPERIMENTS IN THEOLOGY

*Activities and questions particularly for disciples in small groups and Sunday school classes, and other growing Christians. Use additional pages if needed.*

List parts of the creation that are a part of the kingdom of God.

---

Ask a friend, perhaps a member of your study group, "When we say that Jesus Christ is Lord of all, what do we mean?"

---

Discuss with your friend (or group) the similarities and differences in your responses to the question.

---

What do you believe about the second coming (parousia) of Jesus Christ? What differences in belief are present in your group? In your family?

---

In your opinion, does it make any difference what we believe about the second coming of Christ? Why does it make a difference? (Or, not make any difference?)

---

The **Kingdom** as the reign of God is free of human frailties but the church, although called to submit to God's reign, is not free of the frailties of human participation.

How does that statement help us understand the difference between the kingdom and the church?

---

Does this understanding enable us to participate more fully in the fellowship of the church? How?

---

---

## EXPLORATIONS IN THEOLOGY

*Activities and questions especially for disciples called or aspiring to serve as leaders in the church, including teachers, elders, pastors. Use additional pages if needed.*

Read chapter 5, "Christ Jesus, the Kingdom, and Eschatology," in *Theology for Disciples.*

Read the list of comparisons of the kingdom and the church. Explain, in simple language, the difference between "qualitative reality" and "quantitative reality."

________________________________________

________________________________________

How do we witness God working among his people?

________________________________________

________________________________________

Now the more difficult aspect: How do we witness God presently working in all of creation, in all things?

________________________________________

________________________________________

________________________________________

Outline a Sunday school lesson for adults on "The Kingdom of God" which will be at once informative and reassuring—especially reassuring to persons going through challenging times in their faith, family, or health.

________________________________________

________________________________________

List several characteristics of the kingdom which a person could reasonably expect to find evidenced (expressed) in the church, "the community of the kingdom." You may want to add a comment on how you think the kingdom characteristic might be better expressed in your church.

1. ____________________ 4. ____________________

2. ____________________ 5. ____________________

3. ____________________ 6. ____________________

CHAPTER 5

# Christ Jesus

## Teacher, Preacher, Exorcist, Healer

Jesus' ministry was that of **teacher, preacher, exorcist,** and **healer.** He taught a way of life, preached the good news of the kingdom, cast out demons, and healed the sick and diseased (77).

The Man of Galilee in his incarnational ministry as teacher, preacher, exorcist, and healer was also the **divine friend**, sometimes **confronting**, at other times **comforting**, but always loving.

The crucified, resurrected, ascended, and reigning Lord who is also the eternal word, the promised messiah, christus victor, and sacrificing savior is always friend whether it is a matter of his **divine** ***No*** **to sin** or his **divine** ***Yes*** **to righteousness.** His *No* is always motivated by loving holiness and his *Yes* by holy love.

Jesus in his threefold offices is the Word-made-flesh **prophet** at whose feet we sit as humble disciples, the **great high priest** who saves to the uttermost, the **King of Kings** and the Lord of lords whose reign will never cease (91).

## Scriptural Themes of Christ's Atoning Work

*Theme 1.* The first theme is the death of Christ as the **objective, sacrificial offering** that God has made on our behalf (79).

The premise of the New Testament is that only divine life can make sufficient atonement for the transgression against God [Heb. 2:17; 9:26; 10:10; 1 Pet. 2:24; Rom. 7:24–25] (80).

*Theme 2.* The second great theme in the New Testament regarding Christ's atoning work is that of Jesus' **sacrificial love** that **wins us to God.** He is the perfect exemplar of the way we are to live, and indeed, his life and death inspire us to faith, love, and service [Phil. 2:5–8; Matt. 10:38; 16:24; Mark 8:34–38; Luke 9;23–26; 14:27; Heb. 12:1–3] (80).

*Theme 3.* The third great theme regarding Christ's saving work is that of Jesus as the victor over Satan. Because of our Lord's incarnational work, we are set free from the powers of spiritual darkness [John 12:31; Heb. 2:14; Rev. 12:9; 20:2–3, 10] (81).

Jesus paid it all,
All to Him I owe;
Sin had left a crimson stain—
He washed it white as snow.
—Elvina M. Hall, *Worship the Lord: Hymnal of the Church of God*

## Contemporary Aberrations about Christ

Let's consider three modem examples of aberrations [about Christ] that are also ancient:

1. The **Unitarian** aberrational view that Jesus Christ was nothing more than a good man endued with divine power;
2. the **Mormon** aberrational view that Jesus Christ is one of three gods; and
3. the **Jehovah's Witnesses'** aberrational view that Jesus Christ is a second level divinity created by the eternal God through whom eternal God worked for our salvation .... All three of these aberrational views are also found in the church's early history.

Unitarian Christology is somewhat akin to the Ebionite approach (late first century), which held that God chose a very good man named Jesus for a special mission in the world.

Mormon Christology is a **polytheistic** view rejected by the monotheism of the Bible and by the church's Trinitarian explication of this monotheism.

Jehovah's Witnesses Christology is ancient **Arianism** revisited. Arius (ca. 256–336) argued that Christ was not coeternal with the Father .... merely the first creature of God, (84, formatted).

We need to be informed by the church's long conversation regarding the personal work of Christ for the sake of avoiding aberrations that have been already addressed (85).

## Prophet, Priest, and King

Jesus Christ is often referred to in relation to the threefold offices of prophet, priest, and king. In continuity with Old Testament prophets, Jesus as a prophet **spoke the word** of God, but, as more than a prophet, he **is the Word.** In continuity with Old Testament priests, he made an offering to God for the salvation of his people, but as a priest with a difference, he **sacrificed himself** as "the Lamb of God who takes away the sin of the world" (John 1:29; see also Heb. 10:1–14). In continuity with Old Testament kings, he too was lord of a particular people (his disciples) but beyond that, he is the universal **"King of kings,** and Lord of lords" (Rev. 19:16).

The twentieth century German theologian, Jürgen Moltmann, argues that at the heart of Christ's three fold offices is **divine friendship** (89).

## SCRIPTURES

Mark 1:39; 6:6 Matthew 4:23–25; 9:35 Luke 4:42–44 John 15:15

**NOTES**

## EXPERIMENTS IN THEOLOGY

*Activities and questions particularly for disciples in small groups and Sunday school classes, and other growing Christians. Use additional pages if needed.*

Give examples of how you have experienced the ministry of Jesus Christ:

Jesus, as teacher ______________________________

______________________________

As preacher ______________________________

______________________________

As exorcist ______________________________

______________________________

As healer ______________________________

______________________________

As divine friend, confronting ______________________________

______________________________

As divine friend, comforting ______________________________

______________________________

As divine friend, always loving ______________________________

______________________________

Jesus is the perfect example of the way we are to live. Which of Jesus' words, actions, or ministries impresses you most?

______________________________

______________________________

______________________________

Ask a fellow Christian: In what ways is your life different because in Jesus "we are set free from the powers of spiritual darkness?"

______________________________

How is the experience of freedom from spiritual darkness of your fellow Christian similar or different from what you have experienced?

In the book *Theology for Disciples,* three hymns are quoted as statements about Christ: "Jesus Paid It All," "The Old Rugged Cross," and "There's Power in the Blood."

Open the *Worship the Lord: Hymnal of the Church of God* to "Jesus Paid It All" number 410; "The Old Rugged Cross" number 195; and There's Power in the Blood" number 423. List a few of the qualities of Jesus' life which are expressed in the hymns.

## EXPLORATIONS IN THEOLOGY

*Activities and questions especially for disciples called or aspiring to serve as leaders in the church, including teachers, elders, pastors. Use additional pages if needed.*

Read chapter 6, "The Person and Work of Christ Jesus," in *Theology for Disciples.*

Dr. Stafford quotes theologian Jürgen Moltmann: "For in his divine function as prophet, priest and king, Christ lives and acts as a friend and creates friendship."

What are some reasons for focusing on "friendship" rather than on the titles "prophet, priest, and king?"

Write below a scriptural text that expresses Christ's ministry as friend or the creator of friendships:

______________________________________________________________

______________________________________________________________

Contemporary aberrations in beliefs about Christ include the Unitarian, Mormon, and Jehovah's Witness views.

Speak with neighbors, friends, or relatives who are a part of one of these groups and ask them to state briefly what they believe about Jesus. (Or, obtain one of the publications of each group and copy a sentence or two about their particular belief.)

Unitarian: ______________________________________________

Mormon: ______________________________________________

Jehovah's Witness: ________________________________________

Faithfulness to the truth about Christ as taught in the scriptures is a controlling factor in a Christian's life. Also, Christians are called to be thoughtful, kind, even generous in relationships with all people.

What are some guidelines the church can give its members for relating to persons whose doctrines we believe to be in error?

______________________________________________________________

______________________________________________________________

______________________________________________________________

This is a difficult assignment for any Christian: Explain atonement "as the objective, sacrificial offering that God has made on our behalf." (Read "Theme 1"; consult scriptures identified in the quotes from *Theology for Disciples.)*

______________________________________________________________

______________________________________________________________

______________________________________________________________

______________________________________________________________

CHAPTER 6

# Holy Spirit and the Trinity

## The Everywhere Spirit

The way God is related to all that exists is through the Spirit who is the **everywhere presence of God** [Psalm 139:7; Rev. 5:6; thirteen times in Luke, forty-one times in Acts], (95).

We conclude that the everywhere Spirit is God's way of being **actively related to everybody** for the purpose either of leading persons to Christ or building up believers into the fullness of Christ. The Spirit, then, from whom we cannot escape is, according to the teaching of the New Testament, the Christocentric Spirit. The **Spirit precedes** the coming of **Christ, accompanies** his coming, and **continues** his coming. The Spirit prepares the way for Christ, introduces Christ, and teaches Christ to us. The Spirit inspires the human anticipation of Christ, reveals Christ, and empowers believers to be the emissaries of Christ (96).

All persons within the context of their own particular circumstances—regardless of who they are or where they are—have the opportunity to respond to the quiet work of the Spirit. **The Spirit knows no barriers** called wrong time, dislocation, faulty communications, or lack of development. The Spirit has had since the beginning of history; the Spirit continues having access to every person in every comer of the world now (99).

## Anticipatory Faith

God...brings them to anticipatory faith in the same way that he brought Abraham to this kind of faith. Their lives, their ways, their cultural patterns may be far below the standards set forth in the New Testament, even as Abraham's were, but their **responsiveness to the working of the Spirit** is, nevertheless, the birth of anticipatory faith (99).

Those of **anticipatory faith move** into the future drawn to one whom they have **not yet come to know;** those of **responsive faith** move into the future knowing the Lord of the future, Christ Jesus. Those of **anticipatory faith** merely feel after the one on whom their faith can one day be fixed; those of responsive faith know conceptually "on whom their faith is fixed...." (100).

The church's mission is to proclaim the gospel to all people so that those whose heart's are tender to the Spirit (i.e., "those who are being saved") **may move from** the **frustrating dimness** of anticipatory faith **to** the **joyous clarity** of responsive faith. We proclaim the gospel to them so that they may cease **being hungry** souls longing to partake of the

Christ whom they have not yet met, and **become nourished souls** longing for more of the Christ whom they have met (102).

### The Trinity: Spatial Categories, Relational Categories

The question that the church has wrestled with throughout its history is how best to think of this **"three-personed God."** How can we be faithful both to the **oneness of God** taught in Scripture (e.g., Deut. 6:4) as well as to Scripture's thrice personal revelation? (103).

The historic conclusion of the church is that the scriptures teach

- that the God revealed incarnationally in Christ (i.e., the Son)
- is also the mysterious personal ground, source, and fountain of divine life (i.e., Father)
- as well as the everywhere-present divine minister (i.e., Spirit) (107, formatted).

Our difficulty with conceptualizing the three-personnel God is rooted in our tendency to think of God in the same **spatial categories** we use for thinking about individuals, rather than in the **relational categories** we use for thinking about persons. Whereas individuals are known by the space they take up, persons are known by the non-spatial relationships they have (108).

When we speak of the three persons of the Trinity, therefore, we are speaking not of three spatially demarcated individuals, but of **three persons in holy relationship** with each other, devoid of spatial demarcation (108–9).

As an individual, I am here but not there, and if I am here, another individual cannot take up the same space I occupy. God, however, is not like that. Even though God is everywhere, that does not rule out our being someplace, also. God is everywhere, not in the sense that God consumes all space, leaving none for us, but in the sense that God has an all-pervasive presence. To put it another way round, even though we as individuals take up space, that does not preclude God being in that space as well (109).

This understanding is important for conceptualizing the trinitarian life of God: the three persons of the Trinity are not to be thought of as occupying three different spaces; rather, they mutually inhere each other without any spatial displacement or loss of distinctive particularity (109).

### Trinitarian God of the Bible

God is the mysterious I AM who encountered Moses at the burning bush. God is the one who was revealed in Jesus of Nazareth. God is the one who relates to all which is not God. God is Father (i.e., I AM), Son (i.e., This), and Spirit (i.e., Relating To the other), (110).

## SCRIPTURES

Colossians 1:15
2 Corinthians 13:13
2 Thessalonians 2:13–14
1 Corinthians 12:4–6
1 Peter 1:20
1 Peter 1:2
John 16:5–15
Romans 1:19–20; 2:11–16; 5:5
Matthew 28:19
Ephesians 4:4–6
Hebrews 11:17–19

**NOTES**

## EXPERIMENTS IN THEOLOGY

*Activities and questions particularly for disciples in small groups and Sunday school classes, and other growing Christians. Use additional pages if needed.*

God is present everywhere through the Holy Spirit. We know God as Creator and Jesus Christ as Savior. Why is it important for us also to be aware of the "everywhere presence of God?"

Read aloud any three of the scriptures listed on the previous page. What does each tell you about the Holy Spirit?

The Holy Spirit communicates (relates) to all individuals. Read Paul's statement in Romans 1:19–20 and 2:11–16. What about these scriptures is reassuring to you? What is disturbing to you? How does it affect your thinking about evangelizing, convincing persons of other cultures to accept Christ?

We experience God as being present in relationship rather than present in a particular space. How do you experience persons—family members, friends, business associates—to be present in relationships?

Does this help you in your understanding of God and the Holy Spirit? If so, how does it help you? If not, can you state why?

________________________________________

________________________________________

________________________________________

When we think about God, Christ Jesus, and the Holy Spirit—the Trinity—we are attempting to understand something which is inexplicable and to comprehend what is incomprehensible. Some persons are willing to accept an abundance of information by faith; others of us need more "reasons" for our beliefs. Probably, most of us accept much by faith but want to discover as many reasons as we can.

How would you describe yourself? Do you accept most things by faith and not need proof? Or, are you a person who must think things through, even matters of faith? Or, are you somewhere in between?

________________________________________

________________________________________

________________________________________

## EXPLORATIONS IN THEOLOGY

*Activities and questions especially for disciples called or aspiring to serve as leaders in the church, including teachers, elders, pastors. Use additional pages if needed.*

Read chapter 7, "The Universal Work of the Holy Spirit," and chapter 8, "The Trinitarian God," in *Theology for Disciples.*

Let's start off with a challenging question: What difference does an understanding of the biblical teaching on the Trinity make in the life of a person of faith?

What difference does an understanding of the biblical teaching on the Trinity make in the ministry of the Church?

In your own words, define anticipatory faith and responsive faith.

Identify some persons in your circle of friends who are living with anticipatory faith.

Name an equal number of persons who are living with responsive faith.

How does your knowledge of these categories of faith affect your planning for worship, Sunday school classes, fellowship, and personal conversations? (Think of the individuals in each group, as you answer.)

Read the scriptures listed on the Holy Spirit and the Trinity, and make a list of the ways the Holy Spirit works in (a) our lives, (b) in the church, (c) in the world.

Would the use of the "trinitarian formulae" more often in worship and fellowship enrich your congregation? State one way for using each of the following "trinitarian" scriptures: Matthew 28:19; 1 Corinthians 12:4–6; 2 Corinthians 13:13; Ephesians 4:4–6; 2 Thessalonians 2:13–14; 1 Peter 1:2.

CHAPTER 7

# The Church

## The Circle of Disciples

The expanding circle of Christ's disciples came to be called the *ekklēsia,* usually translated as church. *Ekklēsia* is from *ek*, meaning out of, and *kaleō,* meaning to call or summon. An *ekklēsia,* then, is an assembly called out of the general population for a particular purpose or cause (119).

The first **definition** of the church, as **the body of Christ,** places the accent on the church as the ongoing means by which the risen, ascended, reigning, and coming Lord makes himself known in history [1 Cor. 12:27–28] ... (122).

The second definition... places the accent on the **church** as a **reconciled humanity**—a humanity at peace both with God and with all of God's people [Eph. 2:111–22] (122).

The third definition of the church, as **the people of God,** places the accent on its vocation. As God's chosen they are called to participate in God's work through nationhood and priesthood. The church is here defined in terms of its mission [1 Pet. 2:9–10] ... (122).

## New Testament Church Life at Its Best

1) It was a fellowship of those who **trusted in Christ** as Savior and Lord. The church was a spiritual network of persons whose hearts and minds had been captivated by Jesus of Nazareth, the risen Christ (e.g., Luke 24) (122).

2) As people of the new covenant, they were inextricably **bound** together historically **with** the **Old Testament people** of God (122).

3) They were a society of believers devoted to growing in Christ's life. The canon for measuring their life together was nothing less than Christ himself (e.g., Phil. 2:1–8) (123).

4) The church was an organism of divine grace for the edification of believers and for blessing all [1 Cor. 14:1–33] (123).

5) It was the sociological expression of **God's mission to the world.** As such, it was a movement reaching beyond itself to the wider world for the purpose of making disciples. It was a missionary church [Matt. 28: 16–20]... (123).

6) It was a community **waiting** expectantly for **Christ's consummation** of world history. Believers lived in the joyous assurance that "though the wrong seems oft' so strong,

God is the ruler yet." They were not to fret about where history was going because they already knew the answer—it was moving toward the return of Jesus Christ [Acts 1:6–11; 1 Cor. 15:20–28; 1 Thess. 4:13–5:11] (123).

## Realism: The Church's Struggles, Deficiencies, and Corruptions

- Whereas theologically, and for the most part experientially, they were a fellowship trusting in Christ as Savior and Lord, it was also true that some fell short of this experience [Gal. 1:6; 3:1–5].
- Whereas they were the people of the new covenant who were inextricably bound together historically with the Old Testament people of God, the fact was that Paul found it necessary to address the casual attitude on the part of the Roman Christians toward Israel. It appears they had forgotten the importance of their historical connectedness [Rom. 11: 17–18]....
- Whereas the church in the New Testament was the society of believers devoted to the growth in Christ's life,... some in the church were not so devoted [1 Cor. 5:1–2].
- Whereas the New Testament church was the organism of divine grace for the edification of believers and for blessing all, it is obvious that at times it was very much a stumbling block to believers and a detriment to others [1 Cor. 11:21; 14:16, 23].
- Whereas the church in the New Testament was the sociological expression of God's mission to the world, the composite picture of the seven churches of Asia, to which John wrote, was that of a church devoid of missionary zeal [Rev. 2:4, 10, 14–15,20–23; 3:2–3, 8, 15–16].
- Whereas the New Testament church was a community waiting expectantly for Christ's consummation of world history, the evidence points toward the fact that some had lost the glow of that anticipation [Matt. 25:1–13] (124–26, formatted).

The church is a society of **people with** a **new identity** given to it by the grace of God, but it is also a band of **pilgrims** traversing the deserts and rivers of life, climbing mountains, walking through valleys, sometimes falling by the wayside, sometimes failing to follow the signposts, sometimes becoming discouraged and tired and weary, and sometimes forgetting the goal. It is because the church is a band of pilgrims—perhaps we should even say, a **ragtag band**—that it **needs to be schooled** well in its new, divine identity given to it in Christ. If it is not so schooled, it will, no doubt, lose heart along the way. In order for the church to keep on keeping on, it needs to hear again and again the message of who it is by grace, namely, the body of Christ, the one new humanity, "a chosen race, a royal priesthood, a holy nation, God's own people, in order that you may proclaim the mighty acts of him who called you out of darkness into his marvelous light" [1 Pet. 2:9] (127).

**NOTES**

## EXPERIMENTS IN THEOLOGY

*Activities and questions particularly for disciples in small groups and Sunday school classes, and other growing Christians. Use additional pages if needed.*

With at least one other person, read the section of quotes captioned "New Testament Church Life at Its Best" and then make five brief statements about your local church "at its best."

1. ______________ 4. ______________

2. ______________ 5. ______________

3. ______________ 6. ______________

Now, read "Realism in The Church," about its struggles, deficiencies, and corruptions, and make five brief statements about your local church "as it really is."

1. ______________________________ 4. ______________________________

2. ______________________________ 5. ______________________________

3. ______________________________ 6. ______________________________

Ask another individual or your study group: What does it mean to you, positively or negatively, when the church is spoken of as a "Circle of Disciples?"

______________________________________________________________

______________________________________________________________

______________________________________________________________

______________________________________________________________

What do you know (understand, comprehend) about the church which you did not know, say, one year ago or when you first became a Christian?

______________________________________________________________

______________________________________________________________

______________________________________________________________

______________________________________________________________

______________________________________________________________

## EXPLORATIONS IN THEOLOGY

*Activities and questions especially for disciples called or aspiring to serve as leaders in the church, including teachers, elders, pastors. Use additional pages if needed.*

Read chapter 9, "The Circle of Disciples As Church," in *Theology for Disciples.*

It is a blessing for the church to be an accepted part of the culture, even an honored part of the community. It can also be dangerous. We understand the church to be the *Ekklesia,* a people who are "called out." What are a few of the ways that a local congregation can identify with the culture, that is, with the life of the community?

______________________________________________________________

_______________________________________________

_______________________________________________

_______________________________________________

What are some ways that the church remains separated from the culture, that is, distinct from the general population of the community?

_______________________________________________

_______________________________________________

_______________________________________________

Give a brief statement, in your own words, of what you understand the following definitions to mean:

The church is the body of Christ: _______________________

_______________________________________________

The church is reconciled humanity: _______________________

_______________________________________________

The church is the people of God: _______________________

_______________________________________________

Compare your statements with those of another. Or two or three persons may work on the definitions together.

What six elements would you include in the schooling of your local church as as a ragtag band that needs to be schooled well in the new, divine identity given to it in Christ?

1. ____________________ 4. ____________________

2. ____________________ 5. ____________________

3. ____________________ 6. ____________________

CHAPTER 8

# MINISTRY IN THE CHURCH

### Church: A Fellowship of Ministers

The church as a whole is both ministered to by God through Christ in the power of the Holy Spirit, and, in turn, ministers to God, to each other, and to the world. The church, then, is a fellowship of ministers. It is a ministry and it has ministries. The church at its best has a spirit of ministry that characterizes the whole fellowship, and it includes various offices of ministry within the fellowship (145).

### The Church Preaching

Christian preaching makes the eternal Word alive in contemporary words. It is a **labor of love** by those who are **chosen** and **empowered** by the Holy Spirit to **proclaim** in orderly fashion Christ's gospel to others. Ideally, it is the church in action through the public proclamation of its faith by those **ordained** to speak in its behalf. It is Christ at work through those who interpret the message of the Bible in faithfulness both to the literary text and to the Lord revealed therein (131–132).

New Testament **preaching** was the public **declaration** of **what God had done in Jesus Christ** for the redemption of the world. The church was brought into existence by preaching, sustained by it, and extended by it (132).

### *Charismata*, Spiritual Gifts

The emphasis in both of these passages [Rom. 12:4–6; 1 Cor. 12: 4–27] is on the individual member fitting into the life of the church in such a way that he or she builds it up. The priority is on corporate wholeness, not on individual gratification. The *charismata* are **manifestations** of the **grace** of God in **individual believers** for the good of the whole (148).

The question of highest **priority** is, What are the **needs of the church?** and not, What is my gift? The attitude consistent with the first question is the willingness to do one's part in fulfilling those needs. The attitude associated with the second may be that of fretting as to whether the church will allow one to use one's gift.

We begin at the wrong point when we first of all seek to discover "gifts" within ourselves apart from the life of the church of which we are members. The scriptural focus is to consider the needs of the church and then to prayerfully consider how God wants to use us for meeting those needs (148).

### Offices

First Timothy 3:1–7 and Titus 1:5–9 set forth qualifications for presbyters, called *episcopoi* in both of these passages but in Titus also called *presbuteroi*. Fiddes comments: This [*episcopoi*] is a Greek title for leadership borrowed from the Graeco-Roman society ... and by now the these leaders are identical with the *'presbuteroi'* (elders) which is a Jewish title derived from leadership in the synagogue (1 Tim. 3:1, 5:17, Titus 1:5–7). The listing of additional qualifications from the *episcopoi/presbuteroi* means that charismatic endowment was not sufficient for holding such a ministerial office (151).

As the word *episcopos,* meaning overseer, indicates, the primary role of the presbyters was that of oversight. First Timothy 3: 5 speaks of them as having the responsibility to take care of the church of God (152).

### Deacons

The second category of ministries requiring appointment to a particular office of responsibility is that of **deacons,** *diakonia* (i.e., servants, ministers, attendants). Qualifications for holding this office are set forth in 1 Timothy 3:8–13 (153).

While all members of the church are called to be ministering servants, some responsibilities need to be assumed by those who are specifically designated for particular tasks. The appointment of deacons, then, is the way the church has of guaranteeing that ministries that ought to take place in the life of the church do, in fact, take place (153).

### Ordained

Adequate preparation for the ordained ministry requires **charismatic endowment, emotional** and **spiritual maturity,** a **divine call** and **comprehensive studies**—all four. It is not a matter of one or of two or of three but of all four. Whenever the church lays hands of ordination on a person whose preparation is lacking in anyone of these four components, it does so at its own great peril (155).

The tension that we witness in the New Testament between charismatic endowment and regulated offices is one that has always been with the church and no doubt always will..... While the charismatic ministry focuses on God's sovereign prerogative, regulated offices of ministry focus on the church's responsibility under God (158).

Holding offices of ministry, but without charismatic power, leads to clericalism. On the other hand, a charismatic ministry that does not have the benefit of the regulated offices of ministry may be devoid of biblical, apostolic, historical, institutional, and intellectual continuity (158).

## SCRIPTURES

Romans 12:4–10; 10:14–15; 16:1–2
Ephesians 4:11–16
1 Timothy 3:1–7; 5:17
Acts 6:1–6
1 Peter 5:1–5
1 Corinthians 12:4–27
Philippians 1:1
Titus 1:5–9
2 Timothy 1:9–11

**NOTES**

## EXPERIMENTS IN THEOLOGY

*Activities and questions particularly for disciples in small groups and Sunday school classes, and other growing Christians. Use additional pages if needed.*

List the ministries of your congregation to the world. List the ministries of the members of the congregation to each other. In this process, we discover we must decide and define what we mean by ministry.

Ministry (define or describe): ______________________________

Ministries to the world (all our communities): ______________________

Ministries by members to each other: __________________________

Identify three characteristics of the most winsome and edifying type of preaching (a) for your congregation; (b) for your city or town. Do the characteristics change as you consider each of these audiences?

1. ______________________________________________
2. ______________________________________________
3. ______________________________________________

Write below a name (or description) of two of your spiritual gifts. You may be aware of these gifts as a result of a study or inventory you have taken or just perceive yourself to be so gifted.

1. ______________________ 2. ______________________

Are other persons in the fellowship already taking care of tasks that are related to your spiritual gifts? If so, what tasks, ministries, can you helpfully accept in the fellowship?

______________________________________________

______________________________________________

Discuss the requirements for being a lay leader in your congregation. Name three or four essentials for consideration as lay leader in your church:

1. ______________________ 3. ______________________

2. ______________________ 4. ______________________

## EXPLORATIONS IN THEOLOGY

*Activities and questions especially for disciples called or aspiring to serve as leaders in the church, including teachers, elders, pastors. Use additional pages if needed.*

Read chapter 10, "The Church Preaching the Good News," and chapter 11, "Ministry in the Church," in *Theology for Disciples.*

A congregation is calling a pastor. Give them some suggestions about how to recognize or discover evidence of the presence of the following characteristics in a potential pastor:

Charismatic endowment: ____________________

Emotional and spiritual maturity: ____________________

Divine call: ____________________

Comprehensive studies: ____________________

With a member of your family, or friends in the congregation, state what you believe should be required of a person seeking ordination as a pastor.

____________________

____________________

____________________

Outline a process your local church could use in helping a person discover his or her spiritual gifts. Keep in mind that a focus of spiritual gifts is edification of the church.

____________________

____________________

____________________

Each congregation seeks to include new persons in leadership but avoid the disappointment and turmoil that may result when a Christian is given leadership responsibilities and recognition, even though the person does not have leadership gifts and abilities. What are some positive ways to avoid this error?

____________________

____________________

____________________

CHAPTER 9

# THE CHURCH AS A MOVEMENT

## The Jesus Movement

For a church group to think of itself as a part of the two-thousand-year-old Jesus movement entails focusing all its energies on discipling the nations serving as dramatic signs of the kingdom, and growing up in the image of Jesus Christ. To be a part of the Jesus movement is to pool our resources to get on with the missionary mandate of our Lord (165).

## New Testament Type of Movemental Church

1. *A Missionary Church with a Decisive Theology.* A New Testament type of movemental church gives primary attention to the Christian mission. In the New Testament, mission is rooted in new theological understandings. To proclaim that Jesus is Lord, as the first century church did, is a *theological* proclamation. To teach that he is the Son of God and Savior of the world is a new theological teaching. To function with the conviction that all people need to hear the gospel about salvation through faith in Jesus Christ implies a *theological* framework for the work of the people of God. For the New Testament church, the Christian mission was an outgrowth of a new theological orientation; their missiology grew out of their theology (166).

2. *A Nurturing Church That Cares about Persons.* Those who are converted to Christ, as well as others who though not converted are within the church's care, deserve to be nurtured either in the faith or toward the faith, as the case may be (167).

3. *An Interconnected Church.* A church group that does not pursue interconnectedness with all other Christians functions in a fragmented fashion....

The wider church includes those with whom any given church has a great comfortability (e.g., a shared piety, a similar doctrinal emphasis, a common history) as well as those with whom it has great discomfort (e.g., foreign mode of worship, different organizational structures, contrary doctrinal emphases, dissimilar social locations) (167).

## A Movemental Structure

1) is **earnestly devoted to the Christian mission**, instead of being devoted merely to the survival of its own organizational structures;

2) is **infinitely flexible in its structured life** as it responds to the Spirit, instead of being stymied in traditional structures that inhibit the accomplishment of its mission.

3) is **involved in grass roots discipleship,** instead of being inundated by institutional intricacies;

4) is **vigorously related to the whole church,** instead of trying to distance itself from it; and

5) is **guided by missionary models** instead of corporate models (168–69).

### Christian Unity

The *first level* of the experience of Christian unity, then, is the **common affirmation** about the person and work of **Jesus Christ.** ... the essence of what is said is the same.

*Second level* ... is **worship with those of "like precious faith."** ... many "right" ways to worship Christianly.

*Third level* ... is that of **united prayer for concerns common to multiple traditions** of Christians, and mutual prayer between differing traditions for the well being of each other.

*Fourth level* is that of **cooperative action** in areas that require a common Christian commitment, though not complete doctrinal agreement on all matters.

*Fifth level* is the **sharing of resources** with those not of our own primary tradition.

*Sixth level* ... If the church is to have a common Christology based on the Bible, it must, at least in that area, **view** the **scriptures** as the **authoritative** literary deposit of God's revelation.

*Seventh level* ... is the affirmation of the **universal work** of the **Holy Spirit** in the multiple traditions of the one church.

*Eighth level* ... is **scholarly work** that crosses the boundaries between different traditions of Christians.

*Ninth level* ... is both the convergence of understandings and the **mutual appreciation** for **differences** that continue to exist.

*Tenth level* ... is a **oneness** of faith and order, life and work, mission and witness ... unity at the Lord's table; a common identification; a united mission and witness the integrative compatibility of services, structures, and ministries; and mutual love in diversity.

*Eleventh level* ... is **eschatological.** It will take place when finally the whole people of God are gathered at the throne of God, the Lamb (Christ Jesus) being at the center (Rev. 7:17) (175–89, formatted).

## SCRIPTURES

John 10:14–16; 17:20–23
Ephesians 4:1–6, 11–13
Revelation 7:9–12
1 Corinthians 16:1–4
Galatians 3:27–29
2 Corinthians 9
1 John 4:1–3

**NOTES**

## EXPERIMENTS IN THEOLOGY

*Activities and questions particularly for disciples in small groups and Sunday school classes, and other growing Christians. Use additional pages if needed.*

To your mind, what is the difference between a *movement* and a *church?*

________________________________________

________________________________________

________________________________________

Suggest three ways a local church can continue to be a part of the Jesus Movement.

1. ____________________________________
2. ____________________________________
3. ____________________________________

The local church which is a part of the Jesus Movement gives primary attention to the Christian mission. Name actions of a local church that may indicate it is on mission.

1. ____________________ 3. ____________________

2. ____________________ 4. ____________________

Dr. Stafford speaks of eleven levels of Christian unity. What levels of Christian unity do you experience? What levels of Christian unity are experienced in your congregation? Choose with other members of your church one expression of Christian unity you will seek to give in your community this year.

________________________________________

________________________________________

________________________________________

Are there aspects of your life and belief, or the life and belief of your church, that hinder expressions of unity with other Christians?

________________________________________

________________________________________

## EXPLORATIONS IN THEOLOGY

*Activities and questions especially for disciples called or aspiring to serve as leaders in the church, including teachers, elders, pastors. Use additional pages if needed.*

Read chapter 12, "The Church as the Jesus Movement," and chapter 13, "Christian Unity," in *Theology for Disciples.*

Outline a class session, talk, or a sermon on the general subject of Christian unity, using the information in chapters 12 and 13 in *Theology for Disciples.* Use the outline in a class or worship session or enlist someone to listen to what you have to say.

______________________________________________

______________________________________________

______________________________________________

______________________________________________

______________________________________________

A missionary church has a decisive theology. Is your theology (your beliefs) impelling you toward mission? What about your theology may be hindering Christ's call on your life? List two actions you will make to increase your knowledge and participation in mission.

1. ______________________________________________

2. ______________________________________________

What does it mean to say a movemental structure "is infinitely flexible in its structured life?" Are you flexible? Is your congregation flexible? Give examples to illustrate the reasons for your answers.

______________________________________________

______________________________________________

______________________________________________

______________________________________________

______________________________________________

CHAPTER 10

# DISCIPLES IN A PLURALISTIC WORLD

### All of Us Have a God Connection

After declaring that God is the creator and lord of heaven and earth, he ends by quoting with approval a sentence known by the Athenians, "In him we live and move and have our being." Paul is setting forth the idea that all of us, regardless of our religious orientation, have a God connection. It is impossible for us to be other than the creation of God. For this reason, followers of Jesus have a common basis for conversing with others about God. "He is not far from each one of us" [Acts 17:16–34] (193–94).

### The Christian's Approach to Persons of Other Faiths

The foundational question is whether we view Christian claims that God is Trinity and that Christ Jesus is the only divine savior as being merely options among many equally (or unequally) acceptable conceptions of God or whether we view them as being ultimately true. The watershed issue that decisively influences one's approach to people of other faiths is a whether we are convinced that the trinitarian God is the only eternal God (196).

1. The first approach is that of a casual interest in diversity. The basic attitude in this approach is that all of us are historically and culturally formed and that our respective world views, being relative to those factors, are simply expressive of divergent historical and cultural experiences (197).

- Casual interest in diversity points in the right direction, but it is inadequate in that it does not focus on the God behind the diversity (202).

2. A second approach is that of zealous dogmatism about a new concept of God. This approach holds that there is a **God beyond all religious understandings** of God and that all such understandings are historical and expressions of God who is beyond anyone historical understanding. For one to claim that one's own historical understanding of God is the truth for everybody is seen as being absurd and narrow (197).

- I find the way of zealous dogmatism about a new way of thinking about God inconsistent with the trinitarian God who has been revealed definitely in Jesus

Christ—a revelation understood to be the revelation of the only God there is (202).

3. A third approach is the **dialogical search for truth** in which case trinitarianism is viewed as **one among several great religious traditions** all of which can learn from each other (198).

- I find the way of dialogical search for ultimate truth inconsistent with the ultimacy of Jesus Christ who is the way, the truth and the life. This does not mean that we are not to be searchers after truth, but that we search after proximate truth in light of the ultimate truth revealed in Christ (203).

4. [The] fourth approach,... **withdrawal,** [regards] all **other views** of God and the world as being **unworthy of consideration....** (199).

- I find the way of withdrawal inconsistent with the nature of ... the God of involvement ..., incarnation ..., and evangelization of the world (203).

5. A fifth approach is that of **numerical triumphalism** .... attempt is made to get more and more of **those who see reality differently to convert,** sometimes by whatever means, to one's own view .... We have the truth and you do not (199).

- I find the way of numerical triumphalism inconsistent with the nature of the trinitarian God who as the suffering God came to us in the humble and sacrificial life of Christ Jesus (203).

6. A sixth approach is that of **dialogical engagement.** ... one comes to the discussion convinced that the trinitarian God is the only living God there is ... others may see things very differently and that the world is a cacophony of conflicting truth claims, **while committed to the truth claim** that **God** is **Trinity,... willing** to **enter** into a **relationship** of **respect** for those whose truth claims are otherwise (199).

- I choose, then, the way of dialogical engagement because the trinitarian God is a communion of interpersonal communicants who are united in the eternal truth ... God is engaged with us.... (203).

The Bible is the record of the engaged God who calls us to be people who likewise are engaged in the lives of others, people who listen understandingly to all who have anything whatsoever to say. We also, however, are convinced that we have the good news of salvation, and, therefore, are "not ashamed of the gospel" because we are persuaded that "it is the power of God for salvation to everyone who has faith" (Rom. 1:16), (203–4).

### The Values of Successful Dialogical Engagement are:

- all partners feel that they have been heard and understood,
- each party has the opportunity to reevaluate its own truth claims, and
- each has the opportunity to come to grips with the reality of differing truth claims and to improve their understanding of them (201, Formatted).

## SCRIPTURES

Acts 17:16-34 | 2 Corinthians 5:11-21 | 1 Peter 2:9-10

**NOTES**

## EXPERIMENTS IN THEOLOGY

*Activities and questions particularly for disciples in small groups and Sunday school classes, and other growing Christians. Use additional pages if needed.*

List the groups of persons of other faiths who live in your community. (You may want to add groups that claim no faith.)

What are the characteristics of their belief in God and the way they worship?

How does each differ from your belief in God and understanding of the nature of God?

All of us "have a God connection." Name two groups in your community (not necessarily religious or church groups) and describe what you think their "God connection" might be.

What attitudes can we develop and what actions can we take to affirm a positive relationship with persons of other faiths, while at the same time affirming and witnessing to our own faith? How do we do both?

## EXPLORATIONS IN THEOLOGY

*Activities and questions especially for disciples called or aspiring to serve as leaders in the church, including teachers, elders, pastors. Use additional pages if needed.*

Read chapter 14, "Disciples in a Pluralistic World," in *Theology for Disciples.*

Define, describe, or discuss what is meant by the phrase "a pluralistic world." A dictionary may be helpful. What is the nature of the pluralism in the area where your place of worship is located?

_______________________________________________

Six different approaches to persons of other faiths are evaluated: (1) casual interest in diversity, (2) zealous dogmatism, (3) dialogical search for truth, (4) withdrawal, (5) numerical triumphalism, and (6) dialogical engagement (see definitions on previous pages).

Which is nearest to the way you have related to persons of other faiths?

_______________________________________________

Which way of relating may be the most uncomfortable for you? Why?

_______________________________________________

Dr. Stafford says he chooses to have *dialogical engagement.* Describe a few of the personal skills essential to dialogical engagement.

_______________________________________________

Suggest patterns of behavior or personality traits many of us may need to alter in order to relate in a more healthy and Christian way to persons of other faiths (or persons who claim no faith)?

_______________________________________________

_______________________________________________

List three ways your church encourages appreciation of persons of other faiths or persons who have a life style that differs from the Christian life style? Or, list three ways you would suggest your church relates to persons of other faiths.

1. ____________________ 3. ____________________

2. ____________________

## CHAPTER 11

# EVIL, SUFFERING, AND SIN

### God's Will

**Emotional Anguished "Why":**... the anguished why that erupts out of the existential experience of tragedy, difficulty, and pain... not asking for a biblical, theological, or philosophical answer to the question, but simply for a hearing (207–8).

**Intellectual, Reflective "Why":**... asked by those ... at an emotional distance from suffering.... What kind of God is it that allows suffering to take place?... It is a request for an explanation that makes sense of the experience of evil... (208).

### Theological Ramifications

**1)** The goal of creation is not simply that we will be happy, pain-free individuals, but that we will be the holy people of God [1 Pet. 1:14–16].

**2)** The capacity to suffer is inherent in our being created in the image of God who has the capacity to suffer [Gen. 6:6].

**3)** Our relationship to God determines whether the experience of suffering is good or evil. ... we conclude that suffering is good when it is experienced in a relationship of love for God....

**4) Our suffering,** whether good or evil, is brought about by

a) the randomness of natural occurrences that all persons, regardless of their relationship to God, experience (Matt. 5:45)
b) the overt work of Satan (2 Cor. 12:7)
c) the evil work of others (Acts 12:1–5)
d) by our own lack of self control (see Mark 9:42–48)

**Also: 5)** disciples of Christ, suffering ... the result of our decision to take up **the cross; 6)** we ... declare to others the message of assurance that **God has dealt redemptively with sin** and **evil** in the person of Jesus Christ; **7)** we are to be **agents of** love who ... **struggle** and **suffer** along with everyone else; **8)** we are to be sharers of hope who influence others by the confidence we have in the divinely glorious consummation of the whole creation; **9)** By divine design this is a **transitional world....** It is not the ultimate world; the ultimate lies beyond the world as we know it (Rev. 21:1, 5) (222–24, summarized).

## Sin

Sin is both the root cause of evil and the moral expression of it. Whereas evil is both personal and impersonal, **sin** is **strictly personal.** Evil has to do with the structure of the whole created order, but sin has to do strictly with volitional life. **Sin is the human being's basic predicament,** the devil's only commitment and God's central reason for the incarnation and atonement (229).

**Primordial Sin is the sin of Adam and Eve** in the garden of Eden (Gen. 1:26–28; 2:15).... Primordial sin was volitional rejection of God and of God's purpose in the created order and of God's mission. This primordial sin set the stage for the whole of human history (243).

**Systemic Sin** ... the sin of the whole human family ... Romans 5:18–19 says that "one man's trespass led to condemnation for all," and that "by one man's disobedience the many were made sinners." Again in 3:23, "All have sinned and fall short of the glory of God" (243–44).

**Individualized Sin, personal antagonism toward God:** 1) It is *anomia,* (lawlessness, iniquity, wickedness)—1 John 3:4; it does what it wants to do, with no thought given to God or others. 2) It is *adikia,* (unrighteousness, wrongdoing)—1 John 5:17; it pursues its own way regardless of what it knows about God. 3) It is knowing the right thing to do but failing to do it—James 4:17.4) It is **"whatever does not proceed from faith"**—Romans 14:23; it is living apart from faith in God. In all four, then sin is pursuing one's own way instead of God's (246–47, summarized).

**Devilish Sin** [John 3:8] is total commitment to that which is antithetical to God and God's will, purpose, and mission. Human sin says *no* to God; devilish sin is total commitment to do that which is other than God .... Human sin is the act of running from God; devilish sin is the act of attacking God (247).

The sin against the Holy Spirit is the condition of being so **completely committed to the devil** that one is in total moral confusion, **calling good evil and evil good.** Scriptures usually speak of devilish sin in terms of being possessed of demons *(daimon),* (e.g., Mark 5:1–20). This kind of sin is the merging of one's will with the devil's to the point of wholeheartedly delivering one's entire volitional capabilities to him. To be possessed of a demon is to sell one's soul to the devil (248).

## SCRIPTURES

Christ's **salvation** work in regard to **devilish sin**:
Matthew 12:28; Mark 1:39; Luke 10:18; Revelation 20:7-10.
Forgiveness and **redemption from individualized sin**:
Ephesians 1:7; 1 John 1:9.
**Take away systemic sin**:
John 1:9
**Reverse primordial sin**:
Romans 5:12-21; Revelation 21:1-22:5 (248).
**Also**: Genesis 2-3; 1 Peter 1:13-16.

**NOTES**

## EXPERIMENTS IN THEOLOGY

*Activities and questions particularly for disciples in small groups and Sunday school classes, and other growing Christians. Use additional pages if needed.*

Are you presently dealing with the question of evil in our world? (Or, do you recall when you were?) Was the nature of the question you were asking more like number (1) or number (2)?

1. Emotional anguish, a "why" that comes during suffering that is simply asking to be heard.

2. An intellectual, reflective "why" as you philosophically ask "Why does God permit suffering?" or some such question.

What are some ways you can tell whether you are asking the "anguished" question or the "intellectual" question? How can you distinguish between the two types of questions when a friend is asking, "Why?"

________________________________________

________________________________________

Give an illustration of suffering from evil that is occasioned by:

Natural events: ________________ Work of Satan: ________________

Evil of other persons: ____________ Our lack of self control: ____________

Decision to take up the cross:________________ Very nature of our world and life: ________________

Sin is personal. Describe the expressions of sin in individual lives. Do not neglect to identify the socially more acceptable individual sins, perhaps sins that are tolerated in Christian groups.

________________________________________

________________________________________

From what sin has Jesus saved you? Are some sinful patterns still dominating your life?

________________________________________

________________________________________

What does the author mean: "The opposite of sin is faith."

________________________________________

## EXPLORATIONS IN THEOLOGY

*Activities and questions especially for disciples called or aspiring to serve as leaders in the church, including teachers, elders, pastors. Use additional pages if needed.*

Read chapter 15, "God's Will in the Face of Evil and Suffering," and chapter 16, "Sin," in *Theology for Disciples.*

Write one paragraph answering, in your own words, the question, "Why is there evil in the world?"

______________________________

______________________________

______________________________

______________________________

______________________________

Using common words and simple phrases, develop a teaching or preaching outline for a teenage group on the general subject, "This Is What Sin Is" (improve on the title).

______________________________

______________________________

______________________________

Ask a person who is suffering, perhaps someone in your study group, to tell you of ways you can improve your conversations with persons who are suffering. Write down his or her suggestions.

______________________________

______________________________

Or, enlist a person in your group or family to play the role of a person suffering from an "incurable disease." Role play ministry (you or the group) to the person with words and actions that bring comfort, information, and hope. What was the result?

______________________________

______________________________

Identify a way to encourage a person to accept Christ's salvation from each of these types of sin (read the relevant scriptures):

*Anomia,* lawlessness, iniquity, wickedness: ______________

*Adikia,* pursues its own way: ______________

Knowing the right thing to do and failing to do it: ______________

Whatever doesn't proceed from faith: ______________

CHAPTER 12

# DISCIPLESHIP FAITH

## Components of Discipleship Faith

The **invitation to trust** him, the **instruction** to **learn from him,** the **summons** to exercise **confidence** in **his power,** and the **directive** to be **devoted to his will** and way. To be his disciple meant that a person's heart was "strangely warmed" in his presence, but it also meant that one's mind was engaged with his teachings, and that one accepted his way of life and was willing to be engaged in his mission. The New Testament portrays faith in Jesus as being relational, conceptual, confident, and devoted [Mark 3:13–15; 2 Tim. 1:13–14, also 2 Tim. 2:17–18, 23–25; 3:14–17; 4:3–4] (253–54).

## Disciples Will Want to Be Alert to Tendencies to Overemphasize

- Faith primarily as personal trust, with only secondary attention given to other emphases, often leads to subjective experientialism. Pietism and revivalism have to guard against this truncated view.
- Faith primarily as the making of right confessions, with only secondary attention given to other emphases, often leads to argumentative intellectualism. Lutheran orthodoxy and fundamentalism have to guard against allowing this to happen.
- Faith primarily as the intensity of confidence that the Lord is going to do something miraculous, with only secondary attention given to other emphases, often leads to prideful spiritualism. Pentecostalism and the charismatic movement have to guard against this.
- Faith primarily as the sacred tradition, with only secondary attention given to other emphases, often leads to constrictive institutionalism. Eastern Orthodoxy and Roman Catholicism have to guard against this (259).

Christian faith is basically a relationship of trust in Jesus Christ as Savior and Lord, as proclaimed by the biblical tradition. It is the heartfelt desire to sit at the feet of Christ revealed in the scriptures, and to do so in company with the historic community of faith. Furthermore, it is the willingness both to witness for Christ by the way we think, live and the accomplishment of divine purposes…

Or, again, faith is to be related to Christ Jesus in salvation, to be informed by the Christian scriptures in understanding, to be committed to Christian service in life and work, and to be empowered by the Spirit in worship and witness (260).

### The Gift of a New Identity: Salvation

**Salvation** in the **Old Testament** is God's decisive action (e.g., the Exodus) and ongoing work of bringing God's people to a **spacious place** of peace, freedom, service, and wholeness (264).

In the **Synoptics** [Matthew, Mark, Luke, salvation has to do with the **appearing, growth,** and **consummation of the kingdom** of God (264).

In the **Pauline epistles,** salvation is understood as the **justification, sanctification,** and **glorification** of human life by God's grace working through faith. Justification is a legal term which refers to our acquittal before God; sanctification is a religious term which refers to our being made holy for God's use, and glorification is a devotional term which refers to our becoming like God (264–65).

The fundamental character of our salvation in Christ is that we are given the new **identity** of being **Christ-people.** No longer are we to think of ourselves primarily as members of Adam's fallen race, but as members of Christ's body. **Grace** is the **source** of our new identity; **faith** is the **means of receiving** it; **repentance** is the **attitude for experiencing** it; **water baptism** is the Lord's **designated way** for it **to be declared** (267).

### Foundational Sanctification

**Salvation,** first of all, then, is the experience of having a new identify given to us by God (273).

The word **sanctification,** *hagiasmos,* signifies the process of **being made holy.** In the New Testament, there are several dimensions of sanctification, the first having to do with ... God's gift of a new identity which provides a new basis on which God appeals to us [1 Corinthians 1:2, 6:11].... The sanctification of which he speaks has to do with the fact that the Corinthians had been chosen in Christ to be God's special people in the world. It does not refer to a special class of spirituality within the church, for it is the whole church ... which is being addressed ... (274).

- Christians are no longer aliens to God but friends;
- no longer sinners in need of salvation, but believers in need of perfection;
- no longer outsiders to the divine mission in the world, but participants in it;
- no longer strangers ... to the household of faith, but members of it.
- Their unique status in the divine economy is that they are "the sanctified in Christ Jesus" (see also Acts 20:32 and Heb. 10:10, 14) (275, formatted).

## SCRIPTURES

Matthew 8:23-29
Mark 3:13-15; 4:35-41
Acts 2:38; 8:16; 10:48; 19:5
Ephesians 3:1-6; 2:4-10
Romans 3:21-23; 4:7-8; 6:3-4; 9:25-26

**NOTES**

## EXPERIMENTS IN THEOLOGY

*Activities and questions particularly for disciples in small groups and Sunday school classes, and other growing Christians. Use additional pages if needed.*

Disciples of Jesus Christ have both experiences of the risen Christ and a commitment to the teachings of Jesus—the experience and the disciplines. With a friend, list first an experience in Christ and then a teaching of Christ. Do it alternately. Or, divide a study group into two smaller groups and have one make a list of experiences in Christ and the second group a list of his practical teachings. Place the lists on newsprint or an overhead transparency with these two captions:

| Experiences in Christ | Practical Teachings of Jesus |
|---|---|

Read the quotations that remind each of us of our tendency to overemphasize one aspect of our faith. Are you more likely to be one who overemphasizes:

Personal trust—a focus on your individual experience?

Right confessions—a focus on a rational statement of faith?

Intense confidence in miracles—God constantly intervenes to provide privileges for the believer and exceptions to normal experiences of life?

Sacred tradition—commitment to the institutional church or institutions of the church?

Salvation in Jesus Christ makes a difference. Among the ways listed are:

No longer aliens to God

No longer sinners in need of salvation, but believers in need of perfection

No longer outsiders to the divine mission, but participants in it

No longer strangers to the household of faith, but members of it

After each of the statements about the nature of salvation give an example of how your life has been changed (converted) by salvation or examples from the lives of persons in your congregation. As much as possible, identify examples that have been in evidence in recent years.

________________________________________

________________________________________

________________________________________

________________________________________

## EXPLORATIONS IN THEOLOGY

*Activities and questions especially for disciples called or aspiring to serve as leaders in the church, including teachers, elders, pastors. Use additional pages if needed.*

Read chapter 17, "Discipleship Faith," and chapter 18, "The Gift of a New Identity," and pages 361–64, in *Theology for Disciples.*

Give a brief explanation of the meanings of *salvation* and how you or others experience the following aspects of the salvation experience:

From the Old Testament: Salvation is "bringing God's people to a spacious place of peace, freedom, service and wholeness."

________________________________________

From the synoptic gospels (Matthew, Mark, Luke): Salvation is the growth of the kingdom of God.

________________________________________

From Paul's letters: Salvation is justification, sanctification, and glorification.

________________________________________

Generally: Salvation means "we are given a new identity of being Christ's people."

________________________________________

Using the quote from chapter 18 (267), prepare a lesson or sermon using these four statements:

Grace is the source of our new identity.

Faith is the means of receiving it.

Repentance is the attitude of experiencing it.

Water baptism is the designated way of declaring it.

Use words and stories that will enable an eleven year old to understand what you are saying. In a study group, it may be fun to prepare a lesson or sermon together.

Create a list of ways (at least six) that the life of salvation is lived out differently than the life of sin. Compare your list with that of another. Or, converse with a pastor or lay leader of your church about your list. Are you too technical or too broad in your understandings?

________________________________________

________________________________________

________________________________________

________________________________________

CHAPTER 13

# EXPERIENCE A NEW SPIRIT

## Sanctification

**Edifying Sanctification:** The same Spirit who brings about foundational salvation **continues to indwell** believers in order to build up both individual believers and the church as a whole. One could call this **edifying** sanctification. ... the Spirit indwells believers from conversion onward. It is not as though the Spirit brings us to the experience of new birth and then departs until at some future time we invite the Spirit to return .... [Rom. 8], (278). [**Foundational Sanctification: Salvation,** 273–25, 277]

## The Indwelling Spirit

**1)** According to Paul, we would not even know ourselves to be God's children apart from the **internal witness** of the Holy Spirit [see Rom. 8:16]. **2)** The indwelling Spirit, therefore, also inspires Christ-centered worship and fellowship with God [1 Cor. 12:3; Gal. 4:6]. **3)** The indwelling Spirit **produces** the **fruit** of the Spirit (see Gal. 5:22–23), and **4)** is **manifested in the *charismata*** at work in and through us for the edification of the church; ... manifestations of the Spirit **for the common good** (see 1 Cor. 12:4–11).5) [gives] us a **foretaste of future** glory when our bodies will be redeemed [Rom. 8:23] (278–79).

The Spirit, then, is at work bringing sinners into salvation and believers to maturity. After introducing us to Christ, the Spirit indwells us, giving us confidence about whose we are, inspiring Christ-centered worship, producing the fruit of the Spirit, ministering through us for the edification of the church, and giving us a foretaste of the consummation at the end of the age (279).

## Effusive Sanctification

Acts 2 speaks of a work of the Spirit which is not implicit in the gift of salvation. It is an **effusive (pouring forth** without reserve) work. This outpouring on the day of Pentecost catapulted the church into the worldwide mission of Christ (vv 2–3).... The result of the pentecostal outpouring was the ongoing witness of the church ... (1:8). The church was **empowered** both to **increase** numerically and to **live** a **new quality of life** ... (279–80).

It was assumed that the church of "pentecostal grace" would be one of personal holiness and righteousness. The Spirit's effusive [pouring forth] work subsequent to the incarnation was for the purpose of empowering, cleansing, and instructing the church for Christ-centered living and mission... (281).

### Developmental Sanctification

Throughout the New Testament, great emphasis is placed on the re-ordering of lives for the purpose of bringing glory to the name of Christ.... Not only is this **realignment** made possible by the grace of God and the power of the Spirit, but **responsibility** for it also **resides with believers** themselves,... [1 Thess. 4:3–8; 2 Tim. 2:14–26; Heb. 12:1; 1 Cor. 6:9; Rom. 6:19; 2 Cor. 7:1] (281).

### Glorification

In our glorified state of **heavenly existence,** we shall finally arrive at the eternal goal for human life, namely perfect communion with our Lord, nothing whatsoever hindering it. The glorification taking place now as we keep our spiritual eyes on Jesus is a **process** which will never end prior to the Lord's return.... The culmination of glorification takes place only at the end of historical time when the Lord returns; the culmination of sanctification ... takes place prior to the end of time as believers yield wholeheartedly to their Lord (292, 296).

### Issues

The Spirit does not empower and purify believers for witness and service apart from their **volitional response** to the divine offer to do so. The work of the Spirit as indwelling presence has to do with our constitutive life in Christ; the work of the Spirit as infilling power has to do with our missionary life for Christ (283).

The Wesleyans speak of a **second work of grace.** John Wesley used grace interchangeably with the Holy Spirit. Therefore, Wesley speaks of two works of the Holy Spirit. Many who are doubtful that receiving the Holy Spirit is for those who are already saved, might be helped to realize that it is not a matter of receiving a Spirit which they feel they already have. It is receiving a **work not already done** (285).

**Entire sanctification** does **not** mean **flawless behavior;** it means **single-hearted devotion** to the God of our salvation—a devotion which only the "God of peace himself" is able to evoke from us (300).

The crucial issue is the **reality issue. Do we know** ourselves, here and now, to be living in the power of the Spirit for the purpose of Christian witness and service? ... If the present reality is right, one can be certain that the baptism has taken place, but if the present reality is not right, one can be equally certain that the baptism which may have taken place at some previous time, regardless of how definitive and memorable it may have been, is however, no longer valid (288).

## SCRIPTURES

| | | |
|---|---|---|
| Romans 7 and 8 | 2 Thessalonians 2:13-14 | 1 Peter 1:1-2 |
| 1 Corinthians 12:1-11 | Galatians 5:22-25 | Acts 2:1-13; 10:44-48 |
| 1 Thess. 4:3-8; 5:13-24 | John 14:15-16:15 | Romans 12 |

**NOTES**

## EXPERIMENTS IN THEOLOGY

*Activities and questions particularly for disciples in small groups and Sunday school classes, and other growing Christians. Use additional pages if needed.*

The pouring forth of the Spirit on the early church (effusive sanctification), as spoken of in the second chapter of Acts, was for "the purpose of empowering, cleansing and instructing the church for Christ-centered living and mission."

Identify ways the pouring forth of the Holy Spirit is evidenced in your congregation in those same ways:

Empowering for Christlike living: ______________________________

Empowering for mission: ______________________________

Cleansing the church: ______________________________

Instructing the church: ______________________________

Sanctification is often spoken of as a second work of grace; salvation from sin being the first. It is not a matter of receiving the Spirit who is already present, but receiving a work of the Spirit not already done. Four questions appropriate for a Christian concerning sanctification are (answer in words meaningful to you; the questions may be difficult to answer):

Have I experienced the sanctifying work of the Spirit in my life?

______________________________

Does our congregation teach and give evidence of the sanctifying work of the Spirit?

______________________________

Am I seeking the sanctifying work of the Spirit in my life and open to the Spirit's cleansing, empowering and calling?

______________________________

What difference does it make to live in the power of the Holy Spirit? For the individual? In the family? In the congregation?

______________________________

Discuss with your group or family this question: What are the ways we live out *holiness* and *righteousness* in our community? What may be some indicators that we are or are not living *holy* and *righteous* lives? You may have to work, first, on definitions.

## EXPLORATIONS IN THEOLOGY

*Activities and questions especially for disciples called or aspiring to serve as leaders in the church, including teachers, elders, pastors. Use additional pages if needed.*

Read chapter 19, "The Experience of a New Spirit," and chapter 20, "The Culmination of a New Reality," in *Theology for Disciples.*

Dr. Stafford speaks of different dimensions of the Spirit's ministry of sanctification:

- Foundational sanctification: salvation
- Edifying sanctification: the Spirit indwelling believers to build them up individually, and as the church

- Effusive sanctification: the pouring forth of the Spirit to empower, cleanse, instruct
- Developmental sanctification: the re-ordering of our lives

How will you use these clarifying statements to benefit your own understanding of the Spirit's work?

________________________________________________

May these distinctions confuse some? Why or how?

________________________________________________

State two specific ways you may use this information to encourage the people in your group or your congregation to be open to the work of the Spirit and to live in the Spirit?

1. ______________________ 2. ______________________

The *reality* issue is crucial, as stated in *Theology for Disciples* (288). Suggest ways that Christians in your congregation may discern their openness to an experience of the power of the Spirit.

________________________________________________

Some Christians are very humble, even self-effacing, and may judge themselves, harshly. What are words of assurance you may speak to them about their life in the Spirit?

________________________________________________

A few Christians may claim the sanctifying experience of the Spirit but speak and live in ways that do not bring honor to Christ and his church. What is your responsibility to them? What are words of compassion and challenge you may speak to them through a lesson, sermon, or personal conversation?

________________________________________________

Identify three steps that a church which has often been in strife may use to rediscover its calling, the empowerment of the Spirit, and a Christlike attitude, and begin to worship and work in unity.

________________________________________________

________________________________________________

CHAPTER 14

# WORSHIPING PEOPLE

Jesus was not a spiritual recluse; instead, the way he functioned affirmed the crucial part gatherings play in the divine plan for God's people…. We are called to assemble ourselves together not as though worship begins and ends with our entrance into and departure from particular places, but because it is in the gathering that we can be renewed in the worshipful life to which we have been called in Christ. Worship services should be times of rejuvenation for worshiping lives (307)…

## The Lord's Supper: Questions to Ask about Our Worship Services

The holy meal stands at the summit of Jesus' life in the flesh with his disciples and at the base of his atoning work. It summarizes his incarnational life and introduces his atoning work. It is the bridge between the disciple's knowledge of Jesus as an earthly teacher and their experience of him as crucified, risen reigning, and coming Lord…

1. Is **Jesus** the **dominant** presence in our [worship] service, or do we get in the way? [The Lord is the host!]
2. Is the **past honored** as the story of faith in which we, too, become participants? Are the scriptures read and taught, and is the long history of faith celebrated?
3. Is **Christ's salvation** at the **center** of every gathering? Or, is the saving work of Jesus Christ treated merely as one among several possible themes which simply might be the center of services of worship?
4. By participating in the services, are **believers renewed** in their life in Christ? Or, does it deplete them of life and cause them to stumble in their faith?
5. Is anticipation of the **Lord's future** engendered, or is all attention on the past or present? Is attention drawn to the hope that is in Christ for the coming of the kingdom in us, in the world, and in consummation at the end of world history?
6. Are worship services times of **praise, gratitude,** and **thanksgiving** for the goodness of God in creation ... sustaining love ... saving grace? Or ... lamentation.
7. Do the services lead to our **participation** in **Christ's mission** in the public arena? ... is the service seen as a private affair for Christians, ... making those in attendance feel good and wanting to come back for a repeat? ... seen simply as the satisfaction of the soul, or is it seen also as preparation for mission? (310–11).

### More Questions about Worship Services

1. Are we planning and leading services on the assumption that God's gracious **Spirit** is **already poured out,** or are we planning and leading them on the false assumption that we have to conjure up the Spirit?

2. Are the holy fire and the holy wind **preparing the people** of God for **divine mission?** Or, to the contrary, are God's people using the fire and wind for their own enjoyment?

3. Additional questions are these: Do our services of worship get us beyond our walls with good news? Do they have an evangelical consequence? Do they serve as the impulse for committed study, fellowship, communion, and prayer? Do they catapult us into the divine mission in ever widening circles of witness? (315–14).

### Singing

The spiritually robust church will have all three: the songs of the poets, the songs of the theologians, and the songs of the testifiers. It needs the songs of the Bible, the songs of the ages, and the songs of the moment. ... songs of pilgrimage, the songs of revelation, and the songs of experience. ... songs that express the soul, songs that stretch the mind, and songs that rejoice the heart. ... Bible songs, hymn book songs, and chorus songs. ... songs from its own tradition, songs from other traditions, and songs of no tradition (315).

### Prayer

**1)** Prayer is an overflowing fountain of praise, adoration, and thanksgiving to God (Luke 1:29–55; Acts 2); **2)** Prayer is disciplined communion with God..... The Lord's Prayer (Matt. 6:9–13; Luke 11:2–4) **3)** Prayer is the flow of divine energy to the needs of others (Mark 7:31–35; Acts 28: 8–9); **4)** Prayer is the struggle of the soul in relation to God (Gen. 32:22–32; Psalm 88; Matt. 2:38–39; 27:46; 1 Cor. 12:8–9); **5)** Prayer is the human mind seeking the mind of God (James 1:5–8); **6)** Prayer is intercession to God on behalf of others. In a general sense, to intercede is to put ourselves in the place of others and to plead their case before one who can help them. In intercessory prayer, therefore, appeal is made to God who can make a difference for the good (Mark 2:1–12; James 5:13–16); **7)** Prayer is petition to God for our own needs..... God knows what we need even before we ask (Matt. 6:7–8)..... God wants us to ask for that which is good. (Matt. 7:11) ... we are to ask in the name of Jesus. (John 14:13–14) ... we have not because we ask not (James 4); **8)** Prayer is watchful communion with the Lord, which communion keeps us from yielding to temptation (Mark 14:38–72; 1 Thess. 5:17), (325–338).

As disciples of our Lord, we are called to a full orbed prayer life including both the effervescence of its power and the trepidation of its struggles. In a full orbed prayer life we experience both respite and challenge, both joy and anguish, both confidence and questions, both knowns and unknowns, both light and darkness. Jesus invites us to the life of prayer in all its fullness (338).

### Foot-Washing People: John 13:1–20

Having washed their feet, he is now a teacher with a difference; he is a teacher who has stooped as a slave ministering the divine hospitality of salvation (345).

That the practice of foot washing had been established in the early church is indicated in 1 Timothy 5:10 which refers to the washing of the saints' feet as one of the qualifications for women to be placed on the church's official list of widows. That this was other than simple hospitality is implied by the fact that the qualification immediately preceding is that of showing hospitality, and the one immediately following is that of helping the afflicted. Washing the saints' feet, therefore, is identified as a practice distinguishable both from showing hospitality and from helping the afflicted (350–51).

Just as baptism is not a washing of physical dirt from the body, but rather the physical acting out of the cleansing work of Jesus Christ, even so Jesus' washing of feet is the physical enactment of an ongoing cleansing of all that keeps us from being what God wants us to be. Just as the Lord's Supper is not for the purpose of filling stomachs, even so foot washing is not for the purpose of providing physical refreshment, but for giving spiritual renewal to disciples during their pilgrimage of faith (355).

### The Christian Family

The Christian family is a sacrosanct unit within the economy of God. As a little church within the church, it is a place where the faith is lived out, tested, proved, experienced in the most intimate ways, learned, and passed on. When not all members are believers, it still is sanctified by the presence of even one believer in the family unit (see 1 Cor. 7:14). This sanctification means that the family unit is a special arena of grace..... The Christian family, whether a spiritual unit with no natural family ties or a natural unit spiritually sensitized, is the most basic social unit of Christian relatedness (367).

### Full-Orbed

The Christian life is best characterized as that of a full–orbed relatedness including God, ourselves, families, others both inside and outside the church, the whole created order, our particular resources, and the oppressed (361).

The Christian question is always this: How can we extend beyond ourselves and our own self interest, the benefits of that which we have from the hand of God? Christian stewardship has been defined as "the receiving and sharing of God's bounteous gifts, managing them for the best promotion of God's purposes in the world" [Milo Kauffman] (371).

## SCRIPTURES

Matthew 6:9-13; 7:7-8; 26:17-30
Luke 22:7-23
John 13:1-20
Romans 8:26-27
Ephesians 5:21-33
Mark 14:12-26
1 Corinthians 11:23-26; 16:2
Acts 2:1-4
James 1:5-8; 5:13-18

**NOTES**

## EXPERIMENTS IN THEOLOGY

*Activities and questions particularly for disciples in small groups and Sunday school classes, and other growing Christians. Use additional pages if needed.*

The Lord's Supper is a meaningful, teaching, worship experience. It is a theological statement acting out the life and death of Christ, salvation, and the unity of the church.

Evaluate, with an appreciative attitude, the service of the Lord's Supper (communion, Eucharist) in your congregation. Use one of these three evaluative terms for each: (1) somewhat, (2) well, (3) very well.

We partake of the elements of the Lord's Supper often. ______

Our communion services are done with dignity, respect. ______

The Lord's Supper is inclusive of all believers. ______

Our observance honors tradition–historical practice of communion. ______

Christ is recognized as the host and Lord of the worship service. ______

We joyfully anticipate participation in the Lord's Supper. ______

The Lord's Supper renews and energizes our church for mission. ______

Worship services, especially on Sundays with the congregation, challenge us to live for Christ and enable us to be witnesses to kingdom. Suggest what worship has to do with and how it affects the following aspects of the Christian life:

Family life: ______________________________

Financial stewardship: ______________________________

Participation (membership) in the local fellowship: ______________________________

My personal ministry (area of service to God and people): ______________________________

Relationships with people (at work, in school, wherever): ______________________________

Prayer: ______________________________

Read the statement captioned, "Singing." Circle three types of songs which refresh your spirit and best help you affirm your faith (give an example of each of the three you choose):

| | | |
|---|---|---|
| Songs of poets | Songs of theologians | Songs of testifiers |
| Songs from the Bible | Songs of the ages | Songs of the moment |
| Songs of pilgrimage | Songs of relation | Songs of experience |
| Songs of the soul | Songs of the mind | Songs that rejoice the heart |
| Bible Songs | Hymn book songs | Chorus songs |
| Songs of my tradition | Songs from other traditions | Songs of no tradition |
| Example 1 | Example 2 | Example 3 |

## EXPLORATIONS IN THEOLOGY

*Activities and questions especially for disciples called or aspiring to serve as leaders in the church, including teachers, elders, pastors. Use additional pages if needed.*

Read chapter 21, "Worshiping People," chapter 22, "Praying People," chapter 23, "Foot Washing People," and chapter 24, "Full-Orbed Relatedness," in *Theology for Disciples.*

Prepare an outline of a worship service which takes into account the questions we are encouraged to ask about our worship services (310–311). Include hymns, a sermon title with a one-sentence summary, a brief written prayer, scripture lesson(s), and other elements of worship which will enrich your congregation.

Are the worship services of your congregation generally better described by the words given below to the left? To the right? Or, somewhere in between? Mark an *X* on the line indicating your opinion. Be fair but honest, not overly critical.

| | |
|---|---|
| We attempt to produce an atmosphere that persuades God to be with us. | We affirm that God is with us and we rejoice in his presence. |

/ ____________________________________________ /

| | |
|---|---|
| A paramount concern in planning and experiencing worship is personal enjoyment. | The worship experience is viewed as a time to be inspired and prepared for mission. |

/ ____________________________________________ /

| | |
|---|---|
| Our worship services are essentially meaningful in themselves; and not necessarily related to life the following week. | Our worship services provide us with a challenge to be involved in personal spiritual disciplines and in some way involved in evangelism. |

/ ____________________________________________ /

Every church prays, but many seem to use the same words and entreat God to meet the same needs, week after week. Prayer has many dimensions. What subjects could your prayers address which would enrich you and your congregation? Prayer is both elating, at times euphoric, and agony (338). Are there examples of both elation and agony in your prayer life?

____________________________________________

____________________________________________

# LEADER'S GUIDE

*Note: This is copyrighted material. Permission is granted for the leader to make overhead transparencies of "Experiments" and "Explorations" pages for class use. However photocopies may not be made in lieu of purchasing workbooks for each student.*

- **Sunday School:** Often class sessions are planned for thirteen Sundays, one quarter of the year. "The Church" (manual p 28) and "The Church as a Movement" (p 32) may be combined on one Sunday, thus creating a total of thirteen sessions. If it is desirable to reduce to only twelve Sundays, also combine "Discipleship Faith" (p 48) and "Experience a New Spirit" (p 52).
- **Small groups** will not necessarily be restricted to a certain number of sessions. Some groups may choose to continue the discussion of a particular subject for two or three sessions. Conversely, the subject for another session may be covered very quickly.
- Persons **preparing** for **lay or pastoral leadership** and using "Explorations in Theology" *will want to allocate sufficient time to prepare suggested lesson plans or sermon outlines and discuss each issue.* Thorough consideration is the object of the study rather than fast-paced reading.
- **The leader** will read the related chapters in *Theology for Disciples* previous to the small group meeting or class session. Related chapters are identified on each of the pages captioned "Explorations in Theology."
- The leader and persons in the group are reminded that the purpose is to **help each state his** or **her beliefs.** The purpose is not to recite information previously worded by the leader. This is not a class for instruction in doctrine, even though the leader and participants will be encouraged to express their beliefs as a part of the dialogue.
- **Individuals** may adapt the following process to guide personal studies.

### A Typical Class Session

Experience a fellowship of concern. As persons arrive for the session, the leader will greet each one and encourage conversations.

Inquire if there are special concerns one or more persons may want to share with the group–use a quiet voice and evidence a non-rushed attitude.

Ask one or more persons to lead in prayer; the leader will conclude the time of prayer.

1. **Read the scripture,** one selection chosen by the leader from those suggested in each chapter.

For instance in "Disciples: Thinking about Our Faith": the leader will ask, ahead of class time, someone to plan to read John 14:1–7.

2. **Read together several of the quotations.** Not all persons will be interested in every exercise or question, nor will there be time to discuss all the subjects.

   Use different persons as readers of the quotations, from meeting to meeting. For instance, "Disciples: Thinking about Our Faith": The leader may say, "I would like for you to follow as I read the quotation, 'Systematic Theology', and then each of you read in turn a paragraph under the caption, 'Trust, Creeds, Confessions Doctrines, Dogmas, Catechesis.'"

3. **Progress through the "Experiments in Theology."** Choose two of the exercises or questions which you think will be most relevant to your class. Perhaps you will only discuss one, if several want to pursue the subject.

   For instance, "Disciples: Thinking about Our Faith": Considerable time could well be spent discussing one's earliest ideas about God. Many will be interested in identifying the principle characteristics of a disciple.

   **Or Progress through the "Explorations in Theology."**
   Persons who are on the exploration track will give more **extensive** and **intensive consideration** to each exercise and question.
   Persons called or aspiring to be pastors or considering another vocational ministry will want to take time to think through each part of the theological subject and then enlist persons to challenge his or her thinking process and conclusions.
   Persons called to the pastoral and other ministries are encouraged to do both the experiments and the explorations.
   For instance, "Disciples: Thinking about Our Faith": Do each of the four exercises suggested.

4. As the teacher/leader, you will have questions that have come to your mind as you have read chapters in *Theology for Disciples.* Suggest one **concept** or **question** that has caused you to think and ask the group to think about it with you the coming week.

   For instance: The leader may say, "My statement of belief in God seems to always begin with a sentence about how God has met my needs and somehow "speaks" to me about the directions of my life. Is it all right to begin one's theology with a present experience, rather than with God as the creator? Think about that with me."

5. Give in a sentence an introduction to the subject the group will discuss in the next session.

   For instance: "Next time we will talk about the Bible as our book of faith."

6. Pray a brief prayer of blessing; conclude with **The Lord's Prayer**, in unison.

CPSIA information can be obtained
at www.ICGtesting.com
Printed in the USA
FSHW020430260320
68484FS